# STEM

## ACTIVITY BOOK

### SCIENCE TECHNOLOGY ENGINEERING MATH

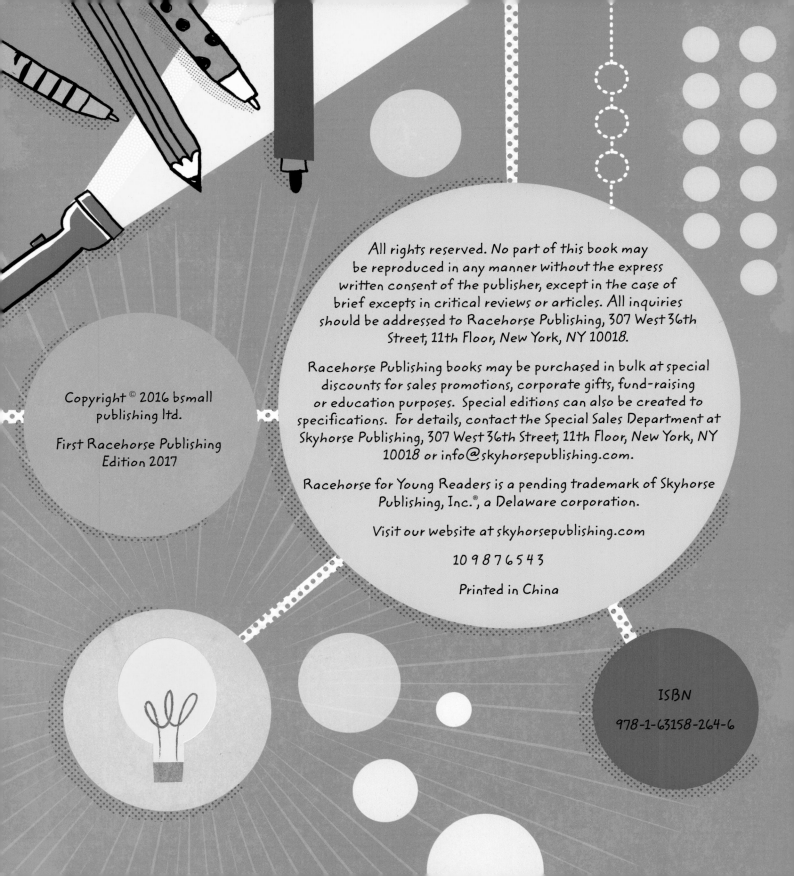

Racehorse Publishing books may be purchased in bulk at special discounts for sales promotions, corporate gifts, fund-raising or education purposes. Special editions can also be created to specifications. For details, contact the Special Sales Department at Skyhorse Publishing, 307 West 36th Street, 11th Floor, New York, NY 10018 or info@skyhorsepublishing.com.

Racehorse for Young Readers is a pending trademark of Skyhorse Publishing, Inc.®, a Delaware corporation.

Visit our website at skyhorsepublishing.com

10 9 8 7 6 5 4 3

Printed in China

ISBN
978-1-63158-264-6

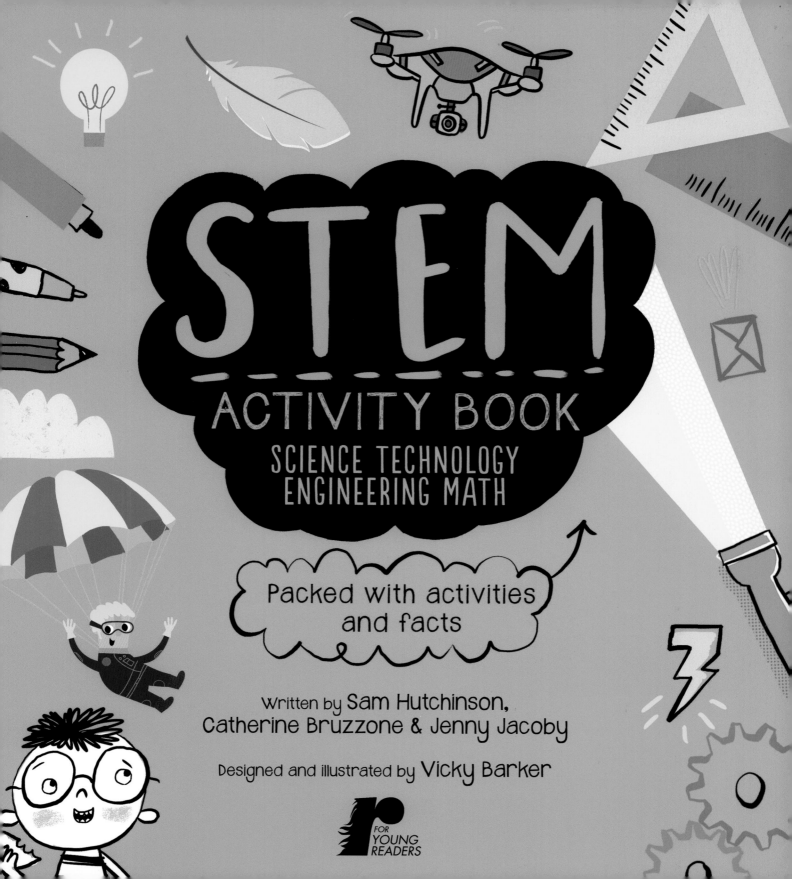

# STEM

## ACTIVITY BOOK

### SCIENCE TECHNOLOGY ENGINEERING MATH

Packed with activities and facts

Written by **Sam Hutchinson,**
**Catherine Bruzzone** & **Jenny Jacoby**

Designed and illustrated by **Vicky Barker**

FOR YOUNG READERS

# CONTENTS

# WHAT IS STEM?

STEM stands for 'science, technology, engineering and mathematics.'
These four areas are closely linked, and engineers couldn't do their
jobs without science, technology or math. Math and science are the
tools that engineers use to solve problems and create machines.
Engineers pay attention to new discoveries in science as
inspiration for new tools they can use to solve problems
in ways that hadn't been possible before.

Science

Technology

Engineering

Math

# WHAT IS SCIENCE?

Science is more than bubbling liquids and test tubes. Science is about trying to understand the world around us, learning from it and using that information in the future. This information comes from experiments that have to follow strict rules so that the results can be trusted. Without strong evidence, someone's idea is just an idea and not a scientific fact.

# WHAT IS TECHNOLOGY?

Technology is the practical application of scientific knowledge by engineers and scientists. Their aim is to improve the things around us. Touchscreen mobile phones are a good example of how technology can make our lives easier. Or the simple and humble door hinge!

Not all technology is shiny and digital. The best inventions are those that everybody can benefit from. There is a lot of technology that is very impressive but that not everybody can afford to use like fancy cars or sophisticated sound systems for listening to music. One other thing to think about is that technology is not always the product that we are using. A lot of industries rely on new technology in order to provide us with new and exciting products. It might not be obvious at first but hi-tech machines are necessary to create things like coloring pencils, chargers or even our favorites sweets.

# WHAT IS ENGINEERING?

Engineering is about finding a problem to solve and finding a way to solve it. Engineers have to pay attention to all sorts of things going on in the world to notice problems they could help with. Then they need to be very creative to find ways of solving those problems. Engineers make things by designing, building and using machines. These machines can be anything from a simple toothbrush (solving the problem of cleaning teeth) to something huge like a wind turbine (solving the problem of finding clean energy).

# WHAT IS MATH?

Math is more than just adding up, taking away, multiplying and dividing. Math is more than just numbers! Math is part of everybody's daily life, from spending money and checking your change, to following a recipe correctly – even finding patterns in the world and sharing properly with your friends.

# OBSERVING ODDITIES

Top scientists use big words to describe their observations properly. They will use words like **OPAQUE** (you cannot see through it) or **TRANSPARENT** (you can see through it) so we know exactly what they are looking at.

Can you spot the objects on these scientists' benches that match the descriptions below?

1. The liquid was very bright, colorful and **opaque**.

2. The hammer was made from a very **bendy** material.

3. The girl's scarf was very **stiff** and difficult to wear.

4. The wrapping paper was **transparent** so I could see the present inside.

5. The cushion was made from a very **rough** material so it was uncomfortable to sit on.

(Answers on page 36.)

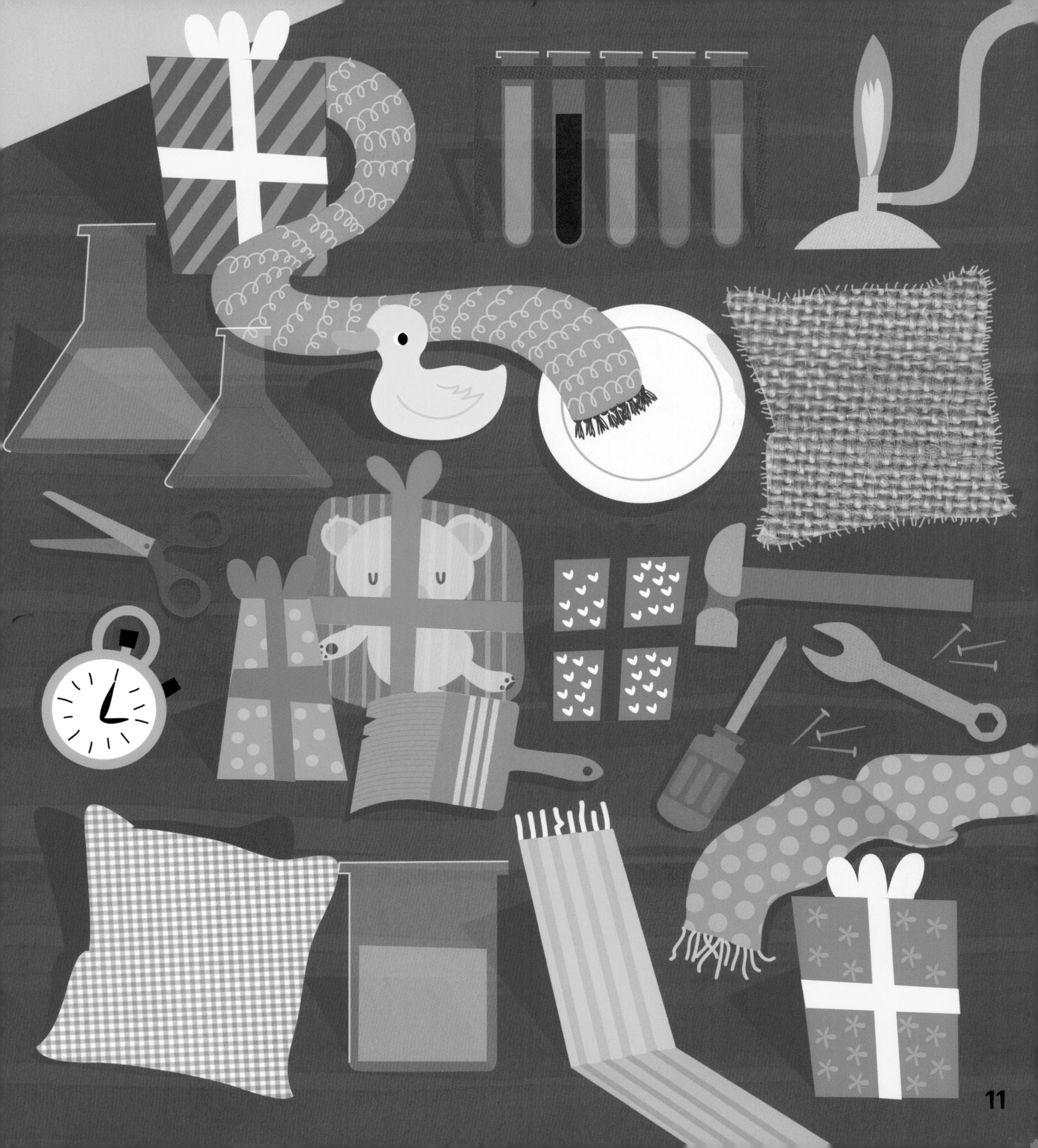

# TWIST AND SHOUT

Materials that objects are made from have their own characteristics. These characteristics are a bit like their personality and help us to decide what to use them for. For example, some materials are very easy to squash or squish or twist and other materials are very hard to squash or squish or twist.

Chair made of wood

Imagine that this person is sitting on a chair made from different materials. Look at the labels and draw the chairs!

Chair made of sponge

Chair made of stone

Inflated beach ball chair

Chair made of cake

# CHANGING STATE

The characteristics of a material can change.
Water becomes snow or ice under **0 degrees Celsius** and it
becomes steam very quickly over **100 degrees Celsius.**

Draw this glass of water
(with lemon wedge to make
it fancy!) next to the
temperatures below.
What state will the water be in?

(Answers on page 36.)

ICE      WATER      STEAM

°**C** = degrees Celsius

°**F** = degrees Fahrenheit

-10°C / 14°F

35°C / 95°F

18°C / 64.4°F

101°C / 213.8°F

# TURNING TURBINES

The turbines in power plants spin to create electricity. The people who run power plants use different ways to make the turbines spin but the most popular method is to use steam. You will see on the following pages the different ways of creating steam in power plants.

The electricity generated by the turbines then travels along power cables to your home and gives power to your electrical devices.

STEAM

Start

Turbine

Find your way through this maze as steam helps create electricity.

(Answer on page 36.)

# OLD ENERGY

Coal, gas and oil are made from plants and animals that died a long time ago and have been buried under soil and rocks ever since. Once these fuels have been burnt to make steam in power plants they cannot be used again. They create pollution that harms the environment.

Spot 10 differences between these scenes showing oil reserves at the bottom of the sea.

(Answers on page 36.)

# NEW ENERGY

Count the wind turbines in this scene.

(Answer on page 36.)

Wind turbines and hydro dams (hydro means 'water' in ancient Greek) use wind or water, instead of steam, to make the turbines in a power station turn. Wind and water are called 'green energy' because they can be used again and again. This is good for the environment. Some people do not like wind turbines and dams because they change the countryside.

# SUN POWER

Solar panels (solar comes from the Latin for sun) create heat from the sun's energy. This sort of energy is popular because it does not cause pollution or damage the countryside. You need a lot of space and a lot of sun to make enough energy from solar panels.

Try to answer these multiple choice questions about solar energy. The answers are on page 36.

**1.** SOLAR POWER PROVIDES A LARGE AMOUNT OF THE WORLD'S ENERGY.

a) TRUE
b) FALSE

**2.** WHICH OF THESE EXPLORER'S VEHICLES COMMONLY USES SOLAR POWER TO CREATE ENERGY?

a) SUBMARINE
b) SPACECRAFT
c) HELICOPTER
d) MOTORBIKE

**3.** ONE OF THE BIGGEST BENEFITS OF USING SOLAR POWER IS:

a) THE PROCESS DOES NOT CREATE MUCH POLLUTION.
b) THE SOLAR PANELS LOOK COOL.
c) YOU CAN BOAST ABOUT THEM TO YOUR FRIENDS.

**4.** WHICH OF THESE LOCATIONS ALREADY HAS SEVERAL LARGE-SCALE SOLAR POWER PLANTS?

a) WALES, UK
b) SIBERIA, RUSSIA
c) CALIFORNIA, USA

**5.** SOLAR POWER COMES DIRECTLY FROM SUNLIGHT. THE SUN IS:

a) A STAR
b) A PLANET
c) A GALAXY

# NEW AND NUCLEAR

Nuclear reactors split atoms in order to generate the heat that turns water into steam which then turns turbines just like in other power plants. Atoms are made of smaller particles called protons, neutrons and electrons. Scientists fire neutrons at uranium atoms to split them, releasing more neutrons and energy. The process continues and is called a chain reaction. Nuclear reactions do not use fossil fuels but do create radioactive waste which is very harmful to humans and other creatures.

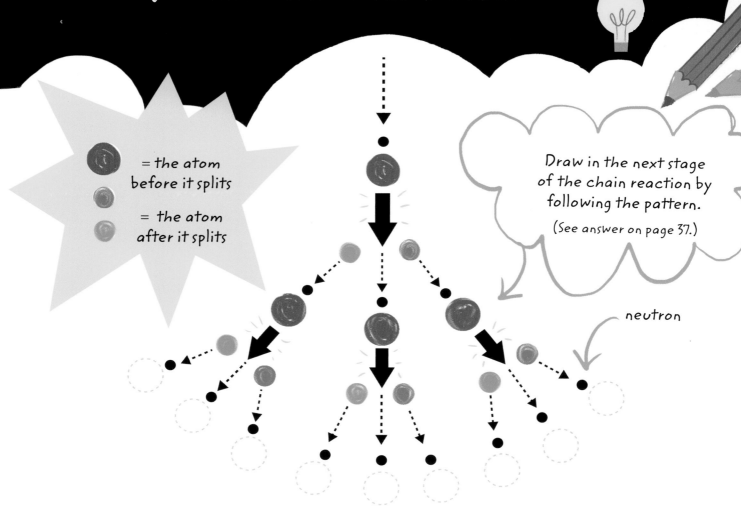

= the atom before it splits

= the atom after it splits

Draw in the next stage of the chain reaction by following the pattern.

(See answer on page 37.)

neutron

# POSITIVES AND NEGATIVES

The circuit on this page has just been connected to light up the bulb.

Electrons are like little packets of electricity and they like to travel from the negative side of a battery to the positive side. Batteries were designed to make the most of this!

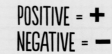

Draw in the electrons running from one side to the other illuminating the light bulb as they go.

Electrons

+

−

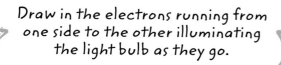

POSITIVE = **+**
NEGATIVE = **−**

Find the electrically charged words in this word search.

| f | w | z | b | k | y | i | q | u | h | j | p | o | m | b | c | v |
|---|---|---|---|---|---|---|---|---|---|---|---|---|---|---|---|---|
| e | l | e | c | t | r | i | r | u | t | n | e | g | a | t | z | w |
| h | h | b | n | e | u | t | r | o | n | d | j | k | s | m | w | j |
| d | w | r | s | x | c | v | b | n | t | r | e | t | t | c | e | g |
| g | n | e | g | e | f | x | v | t | h | c | j | m | a | e | v | e |
| h | w | a | t | l | k | a | a | a | t | o | h | k | o | h | i | v |
| j | k | r | t | e | d | w | b | r | a | s | a | a | u | k | t | m |
| k | m | m | n | c | s | a | a | m | m | p | j | n | r | n | a | n |
| l | f | n | o | t | s | t | t | a | t | o | m | e | k | g | g | e |
| f | h | o | p | r | q | o | t | n | e | s | h | t | o | h | e | t |
| j | k | r | l | i | e | n | e | r | q | i | c | y | n | r | n | y |
| l | p | t | m | c | i | r | c | u | i | t | l | h | w | t | h | l |
| k | p | c | m | i | h | w | s | q | m | i | p | b | a | t | h | p |
| m | w | e | y | t | r | t | b | h | j | v | o | n | h | r | t | o |
| d | a | l | r | y | p | o | i | n | t | e | u | k | m | a | g | u |
| q | r | e | w | c | g | n | e | u | t | r | a | n | r | a | n | p |
| w | t | e | g | s | t | r | m | k | l | y | r | e | t | t | a | b |

atom          charge        battery

neutron       positive      watt

electron      negative

electricity   circuit

Answers on page 37.

# STORMS OF ELECTRICITY

Thunder is the sound that lightning makes. You can hear thunder because your ears pick up the vibrations that lightning makes when it strikes. If the storm is close then you can see the lightning and hear the thunder almost at the same time. If the thunder follows a few seconds afterwards then the storm is further away and the vibrations have to travel further in order for you to hear them.

Lightning happens in the first place when small bits of ice bash into each other in a thundercloud creating positive and negative electric charges. As you saw on page 20, electricity travels between negative and positive charges. This electricity sparks between the two charges inside the clouds or, more rarely, sparks between the cloud and an object on the ground, such as a tree or a building. This is lightning.

Search in this scene for the following things:

- LIGHTNING FORK WITH FOUR PRONGS
- A FLOWER WITH SIX PETALS
- TWO RED UMBRELLAS
- A CAR WITH A BROKEN WINDOW
- THREE LITTLE BIRDS
- A CAT
- A TRACTOR
- A CUPCAKE

(Answers on page 37.)

# WAVES OF SOUND

Sound waves are made by vibrations. The type of sound that you hear depends on the frequency and amplitude (size and height of the sound wave) and what the sound has to travel through to reach you.

Quieter

Louder

Higher pitch

Deeper pitch

Using the key, draw the sound waves to go with these sounds. The pitch is the type of sound.

(Answers on page 37.)

FIGHTER JET

LION'S ROAR

MOUSE'S SQUEAK

WHALE SONG

FART

ROCK CONCERT

YOU TALKING QUIETLY

YOU SHOUTING

25

# SHADOW MAGIC

When there is something between an object and light then that thing casts a **shadow**.

The sun is our main source of natural light and during the day light reflects off objects and into our eyes so that we can see them. Darkness is the absence of light and this means that we cannot see what is around us. Shadows are examples of darkness that we can see.

Our shadow can be long and tall or short and small depending on where the sun is in the sky.

Match these dog owners with their pets using their shadows. Can you guess where the sun is coming from for each shadow? If so, add an arrow.

(See answers on page 38.)

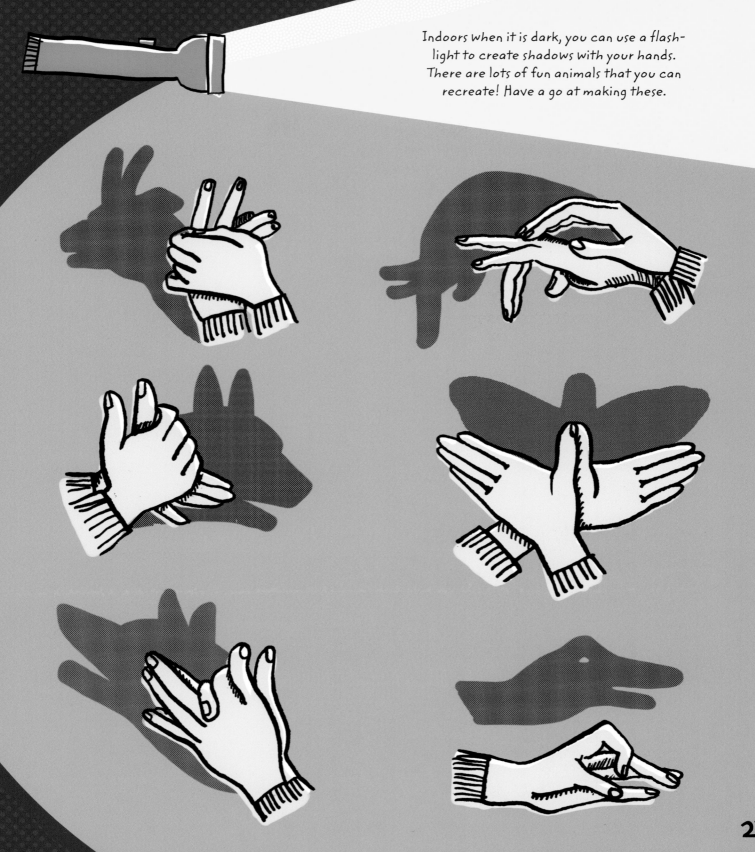

Indoors when it is dark, you can use a flash-light to create shadows with your hands. There are lots of fun animals that you can recreate! Have a go at making these.

27

# WHAT A WHIFF!

Smells travel in the air. The smells are made up of chemicals. When you breathe them in, the chemicals tell your brain what you are smelling.

Choose what these people are smelling. Is it nice or is it nasty? Draw it in the thought bubbles.

# GOOD TASTE

There are thousands of taste buds on your tongue. The food you eat reacts with the buds so that you can taste what you are eating.

Color in this picnic using the following key:

Sweet foods = red
Salty foods = blue
Sour foods = yellow
Bitter foods = green

(Answers on page 38.)

30

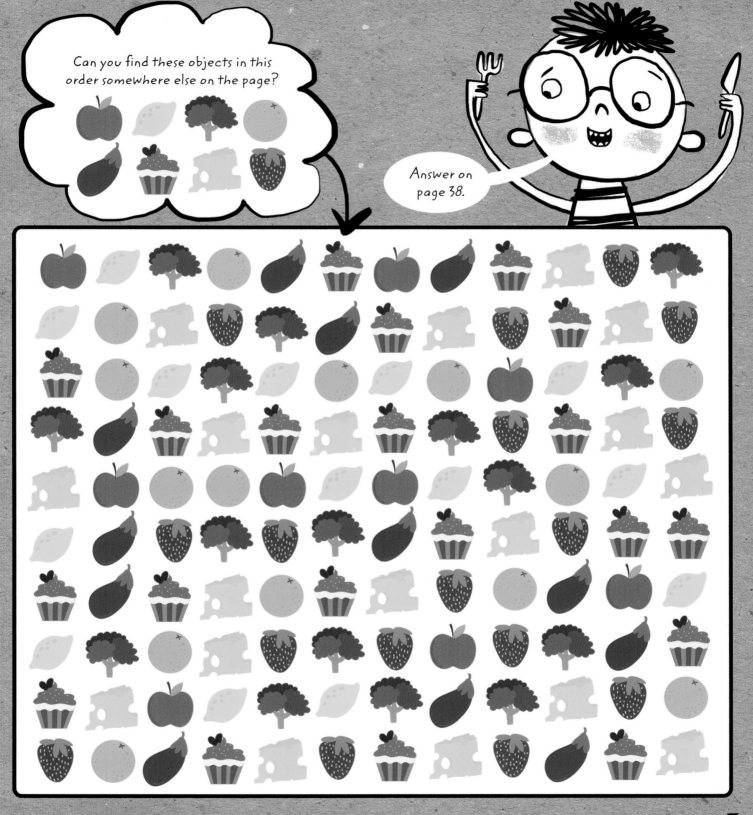

Can you find these objects in this order somewhere else on the page?

Answer on page 38.

# TOUCHING TRUTH

Touch a few things around you now. When you touch something, nerve endings in your skin send information to the brain. They tell you about temperature, how much something hurts and how much pressure you are feeling. Each part of your body communicates with its own part of the brain so that you know exactly where you are feeling something.

NAILS

ICE

RABBIT

JELLY

FIRE

Write down some words to describe how these things would feel if you touched them. Remember, never touch fire and be careful when touching other objects.

Fingerprints can be creative too! Turn these prints into little creatures.

33

# OPPOSITES ATTRACT

Magnets attract metals that have iron in them, like steel and nickel. Materials such as wool, glass, wood or plastic are not magnetic. Magnets have a north pole and a south pole. The north pole will ATTRACT ➡️⬅️ south poles from other magnets but it will PUSH AWAY ⬅️➡️ north poles. The south pole attracts north poles and repels south poles.

Color the north poles of these bar magnets red and the south poles blue. You can tell which is which by looking at whether they are attracting each other or pushing each other away.

(Answers on page 38.)

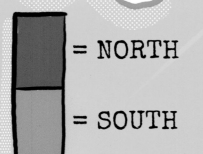

= NORTH

= SOUTH

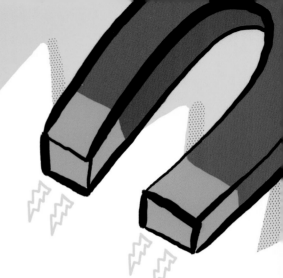

Imagine that you have thrown these things at the very strong magnet above the shark tank. Which ones will stick to the magnet and which ones will fall into the shark tank?
Draw them on the page.
See page 34 if you are not sure.

A SHEEP
A KEY
A T-SHIRT
A CAR
A FRIDGE MAGNET
A CAKE

(Answers on page 38.)

# ANSWERS

Pages 10-11

Page 14

| Ice | Water | Water | Steam |
|---|---|---|---|
| -10 °C | 18 °C | 35 °C | 101 °C |
| 14 °F | 64.4 °F | 95 °F | 213.8 °F |

Page 16

Page 15

Page 17

There are **48** wind turbines in the scene.

Page 18

1. b) False
2. b) Spacecraft
3. a) The process does not create much pollution.
4. c) California, USA
5. a) A star

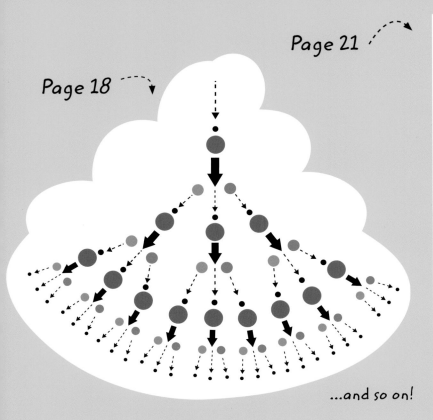

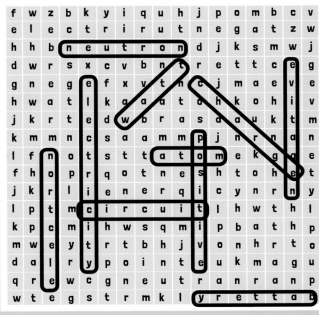

Page 18

Page 21

...and so on!

Page 24-25

Page 22-23

These answers just show the type of sound wave you can draw. So your one might look a bit different!

Page 26

Page 30

Page 31

Page 34

Page 35

MAGNET:

a key
a car
a fridge magnet

SHARK TANK:

a sheep
a T-shirt
a cake

How did you do?

# TECHNOLOGY

# UNDER PRESSURE

We use taps to turn the water on and off in our homes. The taps are attached to the hot and cold water pipes. Inside each tap are two discs with holes in them. When you turn the tap, the discs slide across each other to open or close the holes. The water in the pipes is under pressure. This means it is pushing against the discs in the tap. So when the discs line up and the hole opens, it gushes out.

Follow this safe drinking water on its journey from tap to plughole.

# TOILET TROUBLES

The modern **toilet** means we can flush away our wastewater (poo and pee) safely and keep our neighborhoods clean and free from disease. In the past, wastewater would be thrown into the streets and it was impossible to stop horrible smells. Now when you flush the toilet, the water rushes into the bowl and clears out the wastewater. This runs along pipes out of the house, under the street and to a special sewage treatment center. This treats the water until it's clean enough to go back into the rivers again.

Toilets are very important! Do you know enough about them to answer these questions?

(Answers on page 66.)

1. When is World Toilet Day?

a) 9th August

b) 19th November

c) 1st April

d) 17th October

2. On average, how many years of your life do you spend on the toilet?

a) half a year

b) three years

c) five years

d) twelve years

3. What did the Vikings use instead of toilet paper (which hadn't been invented yet)?

a) a wide stick

b) big leaves

c) sheep's wool

d) animal skins

5. What else does the technology used to make toilet brushes also make?

a) artificial trees

b) toothbrushes

c) rulers

d) plastic jewellery

4. Which of these things carries more germs than an average toilet seat?

a) mobile phone

b) computer keyboard

c) washing up sponge

d) pet food bowl

# CATCH!

Medieval castles and cities were defended by big, strong walls. Before the invention of gunpowder, catapults were the best weapon to attack a city or castle. The arm holding the stones is held down, under tension, so it is trying to pull away from whatever is holding it in place. When the tension is released, the arm swings round and shoots out the stone. Catapults could shoot heavy stones and even rotting animal bodies!

Draw the curving path, or trajectory, of each missile being fired from these catapults. Choose different missiles and see if any of them will hit the castle under siege.

(Answers on page 66.)

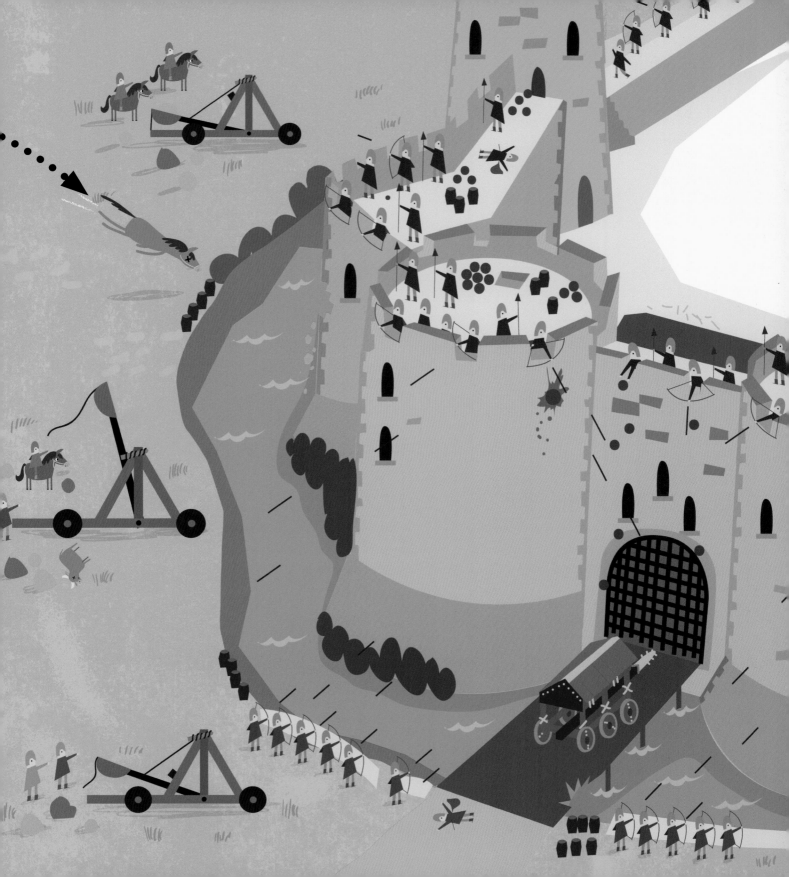

# SPIN CYCLE

Have you tried washing any clothes by hand? It's very hard work. Washing machines automatically fill up with water, add soap powder or liquid, heat up the water, jumble the clothes around so the dirt falls off, rinse them several times and then spin them to dry them as much as possible.

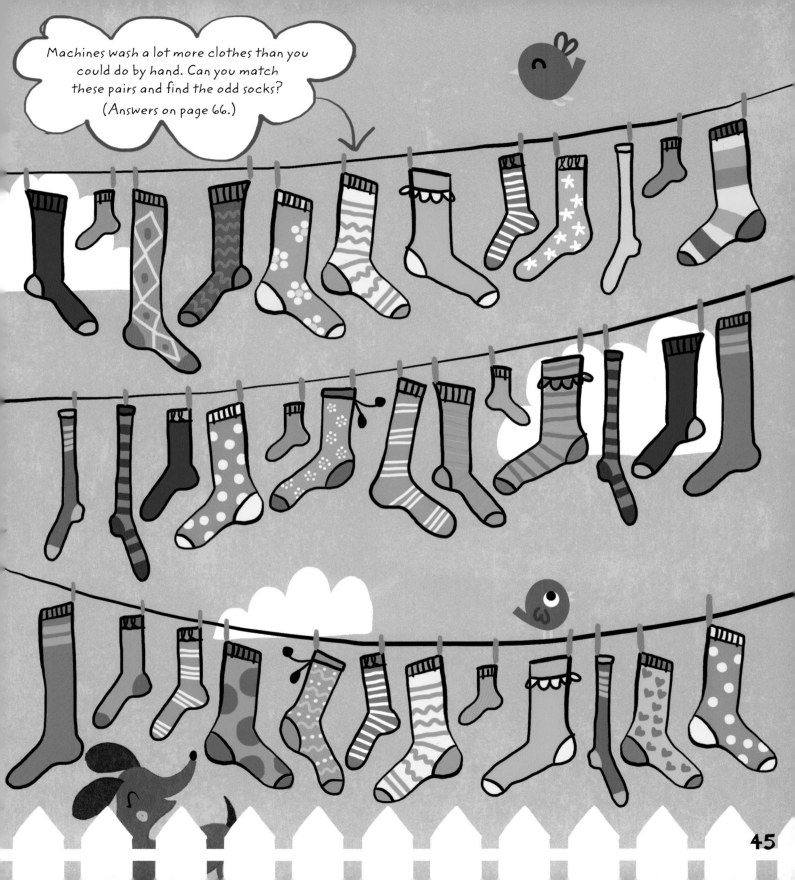

Machines wash a lot more clothes than you could do by hand. Can you match these pairs and find the odd socks?

(Answers on page 66.)

# ZIPPING ALONG

Finish off this zipper. Then decorate the pencil case.

On either side of a zipper is a row of links. These links are exactly the same size and exactly the same space apart so you can count: link, space, link, space, link, space and so on. One side of the zipper starts with a link at the bottom and the other side starts with the space at the bottom so when you zip up your coat the slider (the piece you hold) joins the links together.

Before zippers were invented at the beginning of the 1900s, clothes were fastened with buttons or hooks-and-eyes and it took a lot longer to dress. Rich people even had servants to help them get dressed! Now there are even airtight zippers for deep-sea divers or space suits. This is an example of how simple technology can really change people's lives.

Color in all the outfits that need zippers. Check your artwork on page 66.

# HUFF AND PUFF

When you pull out the handle of a pump, it draws in air. Then you push the handle in and the air is pressed down, or compressed, at the bottom of the tube or chamber. The pressure of the air opens a small valve, like a little gate, and the air rushes out through a narrow tube at a high speed. This blows up the ball...or the balloon or the bike tire.

Unravel this mess of pump tubes to find out who is pumping up their balloon the quickest.

(Answer on page 67.)

Valve

Pump piston

Pump cylinder

Spot 20 differences between these two scenes. The family on the bottom need a new pump!

Check your answers on page 67.

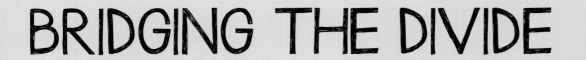

# BRIDGING THE DIVIDE

Truss Bridge

Arch Bridge

There are lots of different types of bridges. Can you get this family from their home to the beach, crossing every bridge only once?

(Answer on page 67.)

Beam Bridge

Cable Stayed Bridge

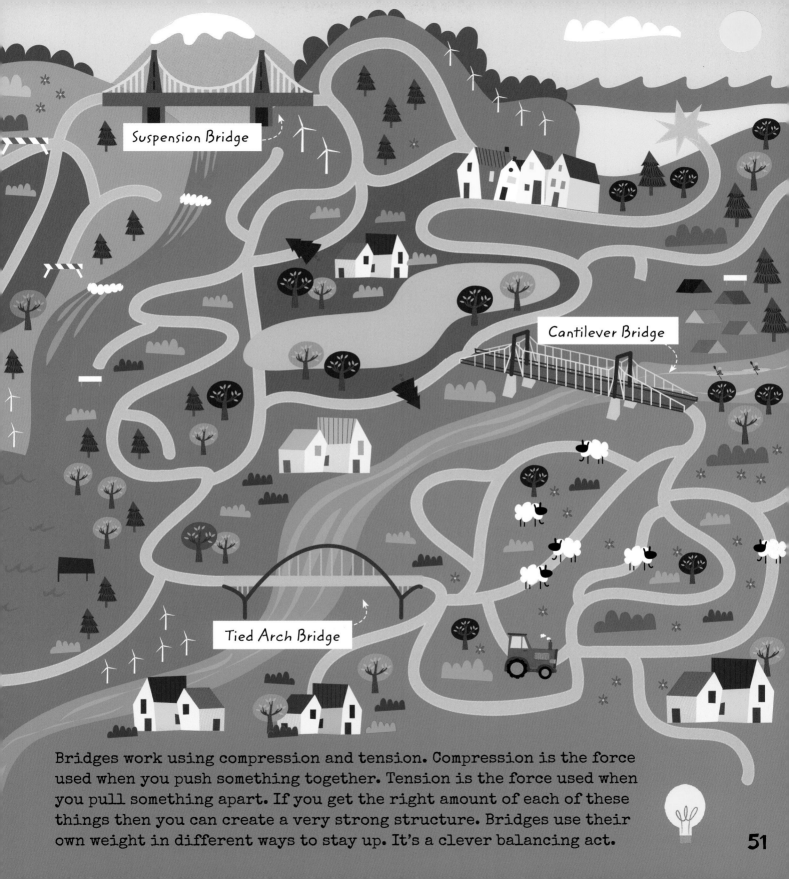

Suspension Bridge

Cantilever Bridge

Tied Arch Bridge

Bridges work using compression and tension. Compression is the force used when you push something together. Tension is the force used when you pull something apart. If you get the right amount of each of these things then you can create a very strong structure. Bridges use their own weight in different ways to stay up. It's a clever balancing act.

# THE WORLD WIDE WEB

What do you think
the internet looks like?
Draw it here.

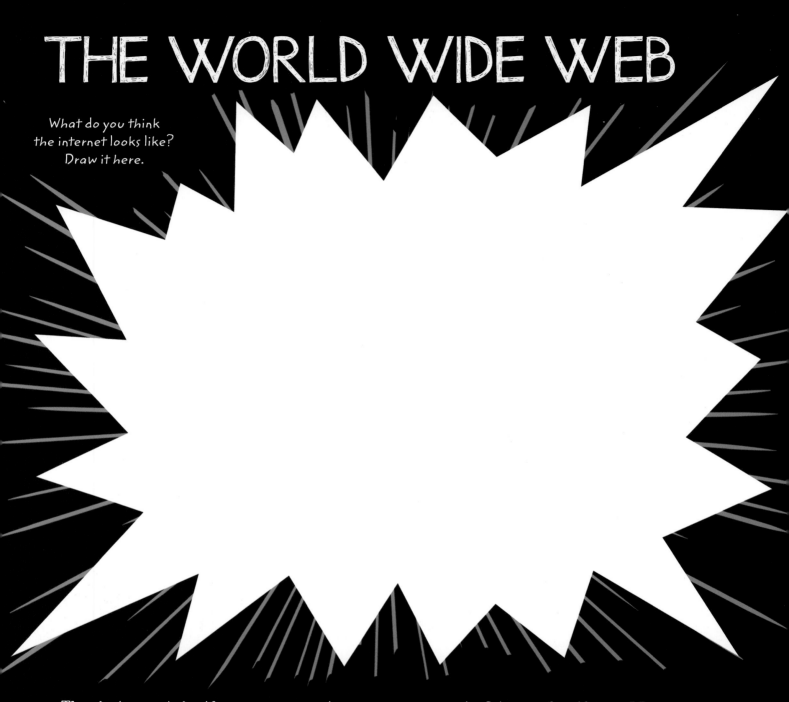

The internet is the way computers are connected to each other all over
the world. They might be linked by wires or without wires, called wireless.
You can use the internet to send email messages, chat online and make phone
or video calls. You can also search for information on the web or world
wide web (www). These are pages of information linked together by the
internet. You find those pages through a web browser.

| | | | | | | | | | | | | | | | |
|---|---|---|---|---|---|---|---|---|---|---|---|---|---|---|---|
| u | s | e | r | n | a | m | e | o | s | j | m | e | r | i | w |
| g | d | a | n | z | q | u | l | n | s | a | f | e | t | y | e |
| z | r | b | h | k | m | k | d | l | b | o | o | k | e | e | t |
| f | o | r | w | a | r | d | n | i | h | s | h | w | n | o | n |
| r | w | o | x | s | s | t | p | n | s | e | v | i | r | u | s |
| e | s | w | e | b | s | i | t | e | h | m | d | y | e | j | o |
| p | s | s | r | h | l | g | r | i | a | a | i | w | t | f | c |
| l | a | e | a | p | g | d | p | k | o | i | k | l | n | p | i |
| y | p | r | j | k | d | g | s | s | e | l | e | r | i | w | a |
| b | e | k | r | a | m | k | o | o | b | e | m | e | i | l | l |

| | | | |
|---|---|---|---|
| website | bookmark | online | social |
| browser | wireless | virus | share |
| address | email | forward | username |
| internet | safety | reply | password |

# SNAPPY CHALLENGE

Before the invention of digital cameras, if you wanted a portrait of yourself or your favorite pet, an artist had to paint it for you. Early cameras were very large and heavy and took ages to take the photo. Now digital cameras are small and light and you can take photos with a tiny camera in a mobile phone.

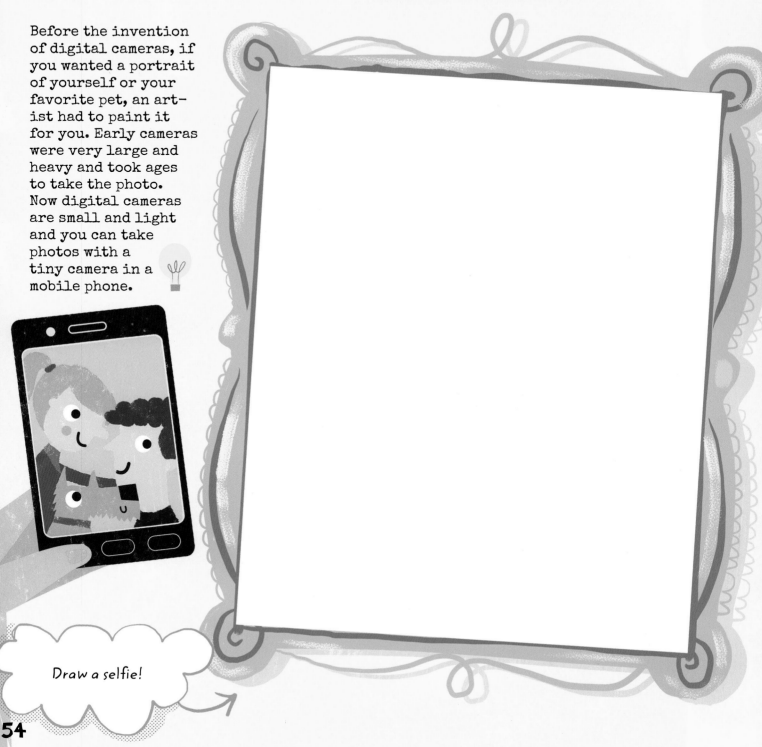

Draw a selfie!

When you point your camera at something, light travels from the scene or object you are photographing into the camera through a lens. This light then hits a sensor, which is divided into millions of little squares, called pixels. Each pixel represents a different color or brightness. The computer in the camera converts the pixels into a picture.

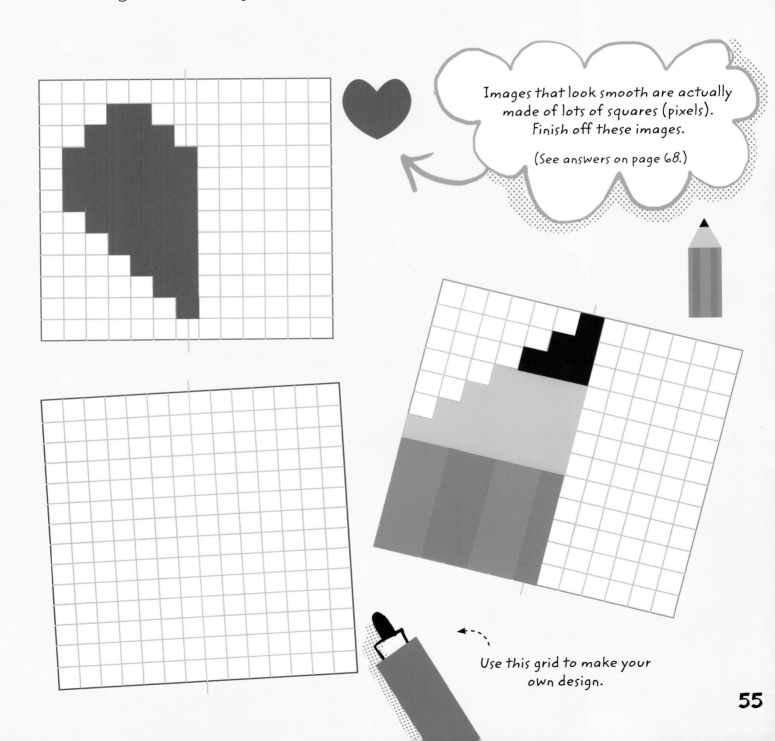

Images that look smooth are actually made of lots of squares (pixels). Finish off these images.

(See answers on page 68.)

Use this grid to make your own design.

# TALKING ON THE TELEPHONE

Before telephones were invented, if you wanted to talk to someone, you had to go to their house or meet them somewhere face to face. Now you can talk to friends on the other side of the world just by picking up the phone.

When you speak into a mobile phone, it sends a microwave to a special mast and this mast transmits (sends) it on to the telephone exchange. The exchange turns it into a digital message to send on to the person you are speaking to, along a cable or sometimes by satellite. Your mobile phone won't work properly if there isn't a mast nearby so there are mobile phone masts everywhere. Look for them when you go out.

57

# SHAKE IT UP

Read below about how these microwaves heat up your food. See how quickly you can follow the waves with your pencil. Make sure you stay in the lines! Time yourself and write your best score below.

Microwaves are a type of radio wave. The wave wobbles the molecules in the liquid part of your food and, as the molecules jumble about and crash together, they heat up. Microwaves only travel in one direction. So that's why the food goes round and round on the tray in the oven, to make sure the microwaves pass through all parts of the food and cook it thoroughly.

# WHEELY USEFUL

Can you spot these things in this busy basketball scene? (Answers on page 68.)

2 x basketballs     4 x water bottles
6 x headbands       1 x butterfly
3 x birds           1 x baseball cap
2 x blue socks      1 x flag

A wheelchair means that people who have difficulty walking can go to work, visit friends, go shopping and play sports. Wheelchairs can be electric and are powered by batteries. Some wheelchairs have large rubber wheels so they can go on snow or into water. Sports wheelchairs need to be much lighter than standard wheelchairs so the athlete can whizz around the court.

# GPS KNOWS THE WAY

Think of the route from your house to your school.
Can you draw the map?

Explorers in ancient times sailed across the oceans using the sun, moon and stars to find their way. They didn't have accurate maps. In fact they drew the coastline of the countries they discovered and created the maps for the voyagers who followed them. Now maps are digital (the information is stored in a computer) and you can check your position on a phone or on a small computer in a car. This is especially useful for ships and airplanes. A Global Positioning System (GPS) calculates your position from signals sent from satellites in space. The signal must come from at least four satellites to be accurate.

# CHOCKS AWAY!

Air force pilots sometimes have to get out of their aircraft quickly to save their lives. They use an ejection seat. First, the pilot pulls a handle and the roof of the plane explodes off. A catapult then pushes the seat along some rails and out of the plane. Then a small rocket fires it away from the plane. Next a small parachute opens to slow the seat down. Finally the small parachute pulls the main parachute out and the seat is shot away so the pilot can float to earth safely.

This pilot has engaged his ejection seat! But these pictures are in the wrong order. Number them correctly.

(Answers on page 68.)

# OPEN AND SHUT

All these things have hinges so you can open and shut them easily. What can you find in your house that has a hinge?

Make a list below. And watch your fingers!

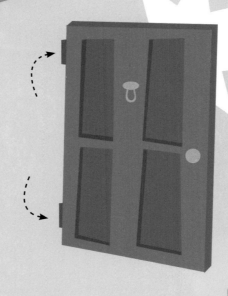

A hinge connects two solid pieces so that they can rotate, or turn, away from each other smoothly. Look for other hinges around the house. We have types of hinges in our body too. Can you think where?

Answer: fingers, toes, shoulders, knees and ankles

# ON THE ROAD

Unlike gas-powered cars, electric cars don't pollute the air but they do need electricity to charge their batteries. They are much quieter than gas-powered cars and much cheaper to run. They can't do long journeys without being charged but most people only do short journeys in their cars anyway. Cars that don't need drivers are coming soon! Can you imagine what they will look like?

Draw a fantasy car. It's an electric car so you have to attach it to the electricity to power it up.

# ANSWERS

Pages 42-43

Page 41

1. b) 19th November
2. b) three years
3. c) sheep's wool
4. They all do!
5. a) artificial trees

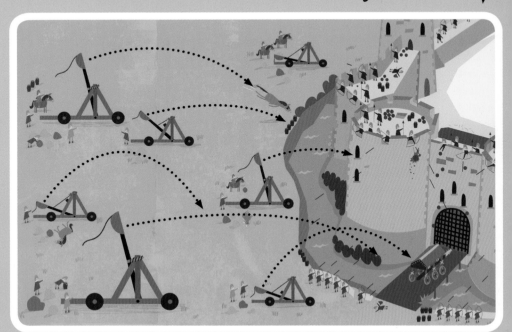

Pages 44-45

Page 47

Page 48

Page 49

Pages 50-51

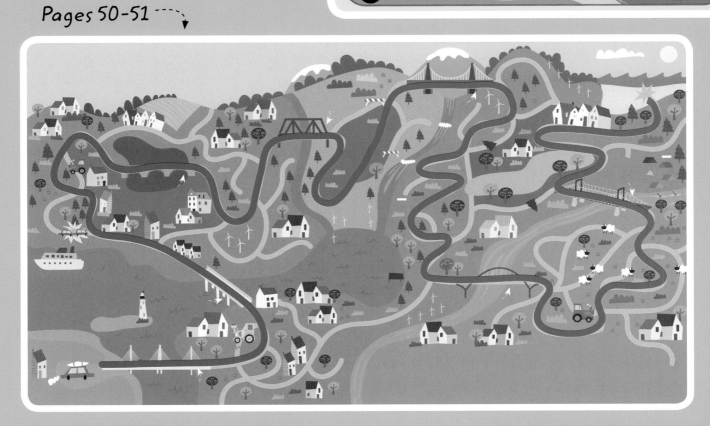

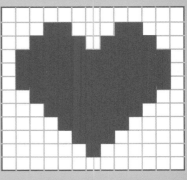

Page 55

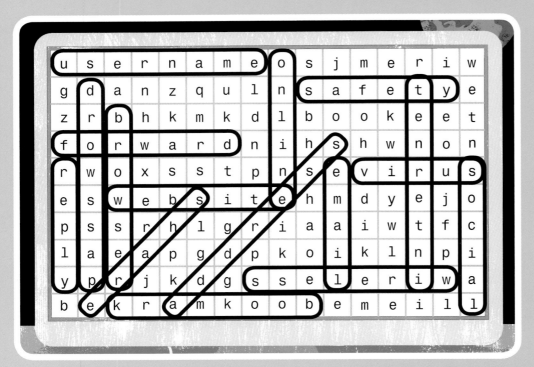

Page 53

Page 59

Page 62

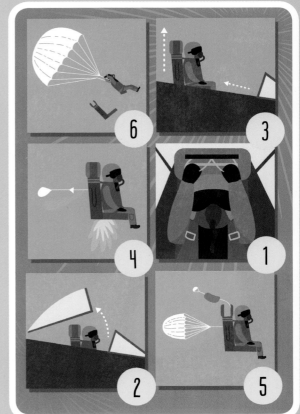

ENGINEERING

# PRINTING PRESS

Back in the Middle Ages, books were hand-written and then copied out (mostly by teams of monks). This meant there were very few copies of books, and each one was very expensive.

The engineer who solved the problem of books being such hard work to make was **Johannes Gutenberg.** His solution was 'moveable type' – lots of copies of each letter of the alphabet, made out of metal, which printers could combine in different ways in a printing press to make any number of copies of any text.

Johannes Gutenberg

## FACT!

Moveable type was used in Asia for hundreds of years before Gutenberg's invention, but because European alphabets are so much smaller than those in Asia, the invention was even more useful, so it spread very quickly across Europe.

Moveable type goes into a printing press **back-to-front.** This is so it appears the right way round when printed onto paper.

Look at these presses ready for printing — the writing is impossible to read! Use a mirror to see what the text will say when it is printed.

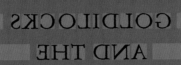

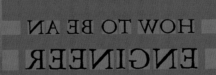

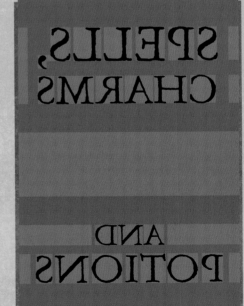

# CYCLING ELECTRICITY

What is better than having lights on your bike when it's dark outside?
Bike lights that don't need batteries to run! Some bikes have dynamo lights,
which are machines that turn movement into electricity. The dynamo fixes
to a moving part of the bicycle (the wheel or the hub) and as the wheel goes
round, it turns the dynamo and that produces an electrical current.
The electrical current gives power to the bicycle light.

The downside of dynamo
lights is that the lights don't
work when you're not moving!

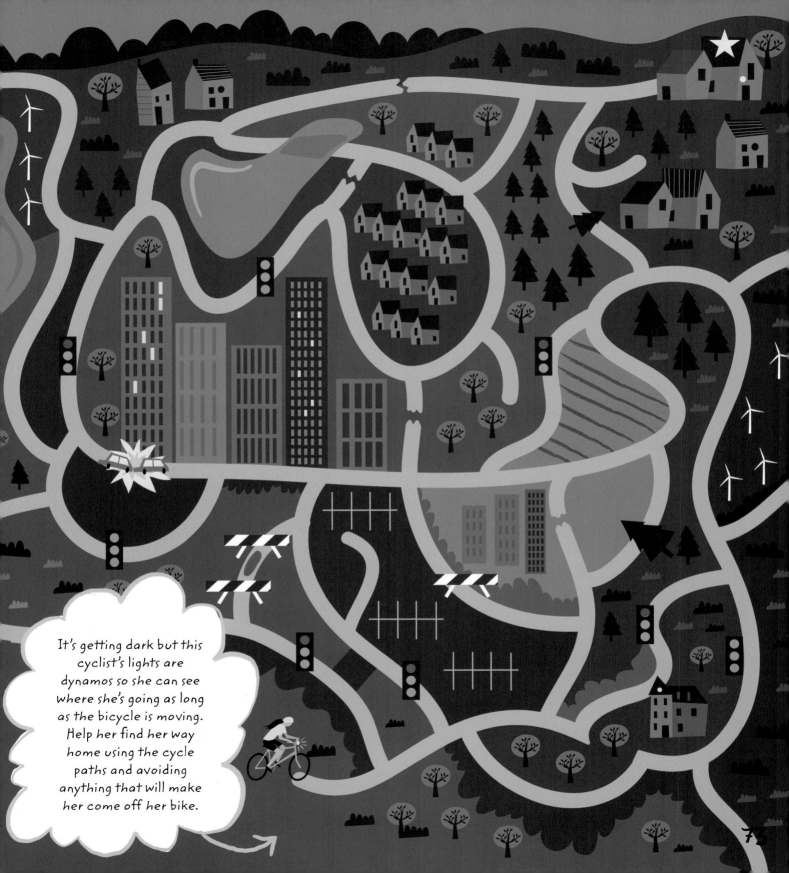

It's getting dark but this cyclist's lights are dynamos so she can see where she's going as long as the bicycle is moving. Help her find her way home using the cycle paths and avoiding anything that will make her come off her bike.

73

# SEE-SAW LEVERS

Levers are one of the oldest machines in the world, and they help to lift things that would be too heavy to lift by yourself. Levers need something called a 'fulcrum' to balance on. By changing the position of the heavy and light things along the lever, heavy things can be lifted more easily.

Something light can help lift something heavy if the heavy thing is close to the fulcrum and the light thing is far from it.

LEVER

FULCRUM

A fun kind of lever is the see-saw. Heavy and light friends can play together if they sit in the right places on the see-saw.

For each of these see-saws, draw the fulcrum in the place that will help the see-saw balance.

Remember: to balance, heavy things need to be close to the fulcrum.

# FLYING PLANES

The problem of how to get a large metal airplane, filled with people and luggage, up into the sky and flying seems impossible to solve. One thing that helped engineers to solve this problem is the shape of the wings.

Airplane wings are shaped like an aerofoil. When the plane travels forward quickly (when it speeds up along a runway), the air finds it quicker and easier to move the shorter distance underneath the wing than to travel up over the bump of the wing. With more air underneath the wing, the wing lifts up, taking the airplane with it.

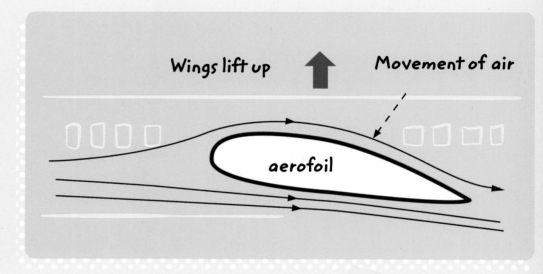

Wings lift up

Movement of air

aerofoil

An engineer who designs planes is called an **aeronautical engineer.**

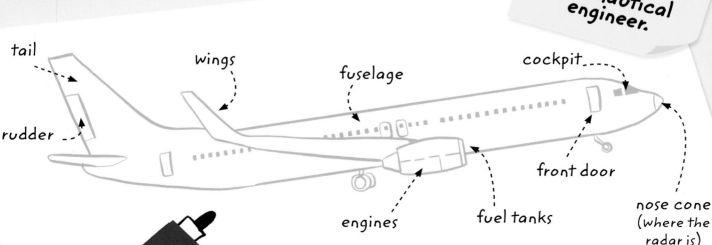

tail

wings

fuselage

cockpit

rudder

front door

engines

fuel tanks

nose cone (where the radar is)

Can you find these aeronautical engineering words in this wordsearch?

```
c j o r v i l d j x e s u o h v e
x o u a e r o f o i l q g x o r i
m o c y i l x v u e l p y z w t h
b e s k o k l g c t e k b x i e i
u a t o p u b r a d a r d s n u o
l n o i t i u b k c e h l i g b t
k f z y j l t t j l v e t l u b a
h y w i l n u r c d u p l m v u i
e c v x t g j e n g i n e a r d l
a r s u i o p o k l o v u k m o p
d e t u m c u i o p l r u d d e r
c y o p u k a n k y k d r x y t m
s t j v o b c p z t i j n o k l o
d s y i b y f d t l h p o m j l v
e y v y r s k u j a m p o c e y m
f u s e l a g e v n i o c r i y j
m t j v h d o u e u p n v t x u l
```

**aerofoil**

**bulkhead**

**captain**

**cockpit**

**engine**

**fuselage**

**radar**

**rudder**

**tail**

**wing**

Answers on page 96.

77

# PARACHUTES

Parachutes solve the problem of slowing down a falling person so they can land safely. They do this by increasing the person's air resistance.

When a person jumps out of an airplane gravity pulls them down to earth and air resistance slows them down. A person without a parachute has very little air resistance, and falls very fast. Because parachutes make such a large canopy, they collect a lot of air, and that increases air resistance, which slows the fall – so the person can land safely.

GRAVITY

AIR RESISTANCE

# ROLLERCOASTERS

Although rollercoasters throw you up and down hills at thrilling speeds, engineers have worked out how to make the ride go by itself, without the power of an engine. Actually, engines turn on just once in a rollercoaster ride – to pull the rollercoaster up the first hill. After that, natural forces power the ride.

Once the rollercoaster is past the top of the first hill, gravity takes over and pulls the riders the rest of the way.

When the rollercoaster starts going down that first drop, it goes so fast it gathers enough energy to send it all the way up the next hill – and so on, as it whizzes around the whole ride. At the end of the ride, the rollercoaster needs to put on the brakes to get rid of the energy and stop the ride.

The rollercoaster goes downhill faster than it goes uphill. Color in these rollercoaster cars in green if they are going fast, and red if they are going slower.

# GLOW STICKS

Glow sticks are great fun for parties but they only last for a few hours. There are three ingredients inside a glow stick and as soon as they mix together it starts to glow. How do engineers solve the problem of the glow sticks glowing before someone is ready to use them? They keep one of the ingredients separate from the others in a small glass tube. When you want to make the stick glow, you snap the tube and shake – this mixes all three ingredients together.

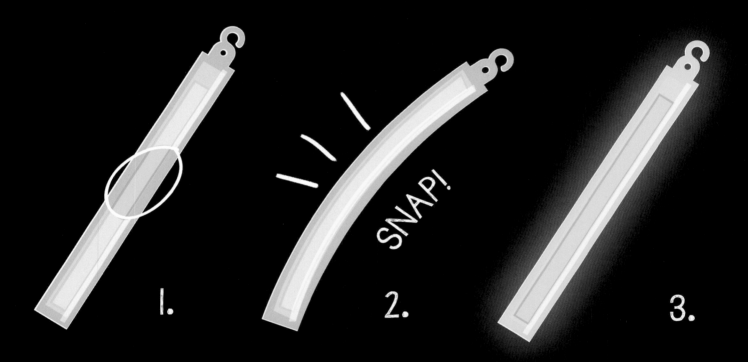

SNAP!

1.

2.

3.

When chemicals mix together and give off light it is called **chemiluminescence.**

An engineer who solves problems with chemistry is called a **chemical engineer.**

Search in this scene for:

- 6 pink glow sticks
- 9 yellow glow sticks
- 7 green glow sticks
- 5 blue glow sticks

(Answers on page 97.)

# EARTHQUAKE PROOF

Some parts of the world have lots of earthquakes. Engineers have thought of ways to stop buildings from falling down even when the ground gives them a good shake. The most dangerous thing about an earthquake is falling buildings. People can survive being on quaking ground but they are in danger if a building falls on them. One way to 'earthquake-proof' a building is to let it be able to wobble with the quake. The more it can wobble, the less likely it is to fall down and injure people.

Look at these three buildings made from different material. Which one will survive being shaken best?

Jelly

Sticks

Brick

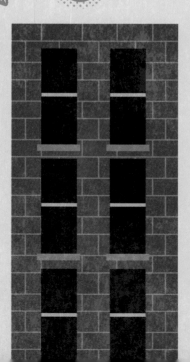

Spot 10 differences between these before and after pictures of an earthquake.

# ECO PACKAGING

A problem facing us all is what to do with packaging when we don't need it anymore. Engineers have come up with some clever ways to reduce the amount of packaging we throw away and the amount of rubbish that builds up on the planet. One way of doing this is by making packaging from reused materials. But the best type of packaging breaks down by itself when you throw it away – this is called 'biodegradable material.' Some packaging even has seeds built into it, so if the packaging is buried the seeds can grow in the ground.

Imagine some packaging for these items. Make sure there is no unnecessary waste and that the materials are recyclable. Draw the packaging on the page.

six eggs

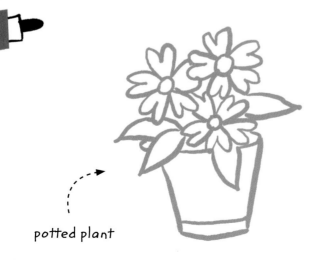

potted plant

a pair of
sneakers

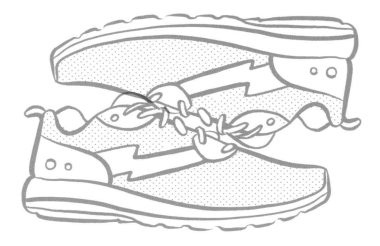

a lightbulb

a soccer ball

a fish

# RUNNING BLADES

Engineers have helped people without lower legs solve the problem of how to walk and run. Running blades don't look like normal legs, ankles and feet but they can make people run just as well as – and maybe even faster than – non-disabled runners. They are made from a very strong but light material called carbon fibre and the way they are shaped makes them bendy like a spring. This springiness helps the runner to sprint forwards in the same way as a natural leg does.

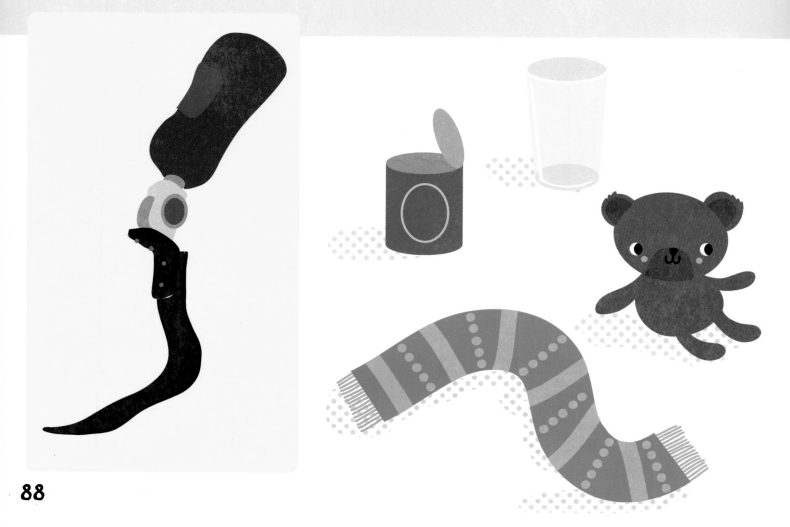

Can you find materials in this selection that might be useful for an engineer making a running blade?

Circle all the objects that are strong in **black.**

Circle all the objects that are flexible in **red.**

Circle all the objects that are light in **blue.**

# DRONING ON

A drone is a sort of robot that can do its job without a human being there with it. There are drones that work on land and sea but flying drones are becoming more and more popular because they are so useful. A flying robot with a camera attached to it can get to places and see things that humans cannot – and it can do it more quietly than a human in a helicopter!

Contains a GPS chip to find locations, an altimeter to tell its height, and an ultrasound scanner to tell how close it is to the ground

Controlled by radio waves or Wi-Fi

Four propellers for stability and to carry more

camera

Can you work out which of these jobs a flying drone can do and which are made up? The answers start on page 96.

Cook a three-course meal.

Tell farmers which of their crops are not growing properly.

Do your homework.

Help to stop people poaching endangered species.

Help to build a high-rise building.

Put out forest fires.

Shop for clothes.

Brush your teeth for you.

Deliver pizza.

Help to save lives.

Play football.

Film long views from high in the sky for Hollywood films.

Do laundry.

Take selfies.

# COMPUTER ENGINEERING

Computer engineers design and build computers to help make our lives easier in a huge number of ways. Computers are part of our everyday lives – not just the computers you write and play on, household devices like washing machines and digital radios have computers inside them as well.

Computers can't think for themselves – they can only do what they are told to do. That means the computer engineers have to do all the thinking first and make sure they give computers the right set of instructions, and in the right order. If there are mistakes in any of the steps, things can go very wrong.

This computer has been given instructions for getting dressed in the morning – but the instructions are in the wrong order! Draw the clothes onto the person opposite in the order the computer suggests. How do they look?

1. Put on shoes.
2. Put on jumper.
3. Put on jeans.
4. Put on T-shirt.
5. Put on underwear.
6. Put on vest.
7. Put on socks.

# CODING

Coding is the way of giving instructions to a computer. It's a bit like talking to the computer in its own language. There are two main steps to coding. First, you need to think about the thing you want the computer to do. This could be something like getting dressed in the morning or finding the quickest route to a place. Then you need to break down that thing into a series of instructions. Most importantly, they need to be in the right order, as you saw on the page before.

Think about making a cheese sandwich with six ingredients:

2 slices of bread

mayonnaise

1 lettuce leaf

1 slice of tomato

1 slice of cheese

Tell the computer which order to use the ingredients in.

94

Can you find these sandwich ingredients in the right order in this set?

# ANSWERS

Pages 70-71

Little Red Riding Hood

How to be an Engineer

Spells, Charms and Potions

Goldilocks and the Three Bears

The Buildings of Ancient Egypt

page 73

page 75

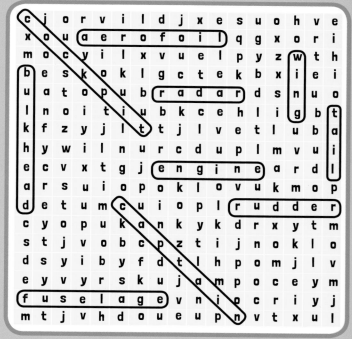

page 77

page 79

page 80-81

page 84-85

The jelly building will survive being shaken best.

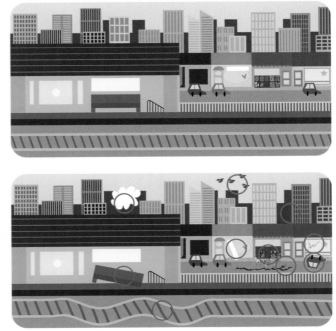

page 82-83

page 88-89

page 91

True answers with some more information:

- **Tell farmers which of their crops are not growing properly.**
  Drones can fly over large areas of farmland to get a better look at how crops are growing, more easily and quickly than a farmer could.
- **Film long views from high in the sky for Hollywood films.**
  Without drones, filming like this would take a lot more equipment and time.
- **Help to build a high-rise building.**
  Drones can carry cable high up buildings and even weave them to help build a structure.
- **Put out wild fires.**
  Drones can fly to spot wildfires and use special cameras to see through fire smoke, giving information to firefighters about the size of the blaze.
- **Help to stop people poaching endangered species.**
  Drones can keep track of groups of endangered animals by flying closer than a human could but keeping enough of a distance to not disturb the animals.
- **Help to save lives.**
  Sometimes drones can deliver life-saving medical equipment faster than an ambulance could get there.
- **Deliver pizza.**
  Drones can sometimes deliver more quickly than someone on a moped, and deliver pizza while it is still hot.
- **Take selfies.**
  With a camera a drone can move to the right place to take a perfect selfie!

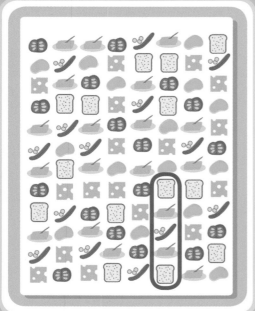

page 95

# MEASURING AND GUESSING

There are lots of ways to measure lengths. You can use a ruler or tape measure to measure accurately, or you can estimate – which is a bit like clever guessing. Estimating takes practice but there are some tricks to help you.

Take a look at these shapes and use the guide to estimate their sizes. The pencils and tomatoes are the correct size on the page so you can use a ruler to check your estimate.

## Symbols

=

This sign means 'equal to' and is used when measuring accurately.

≈

This sign means 'approximately equal to' and is used when estimating measurements.

## Guide

1 cm ≈ the width of a pencil

3 cm ≈ the length of a cherry tomato

1 m ≈ the width of a single bed

2 m ≈ the height of a door in a house

Estimate : _____

Measurement: _____

Estimate : _____

Measurement: _____

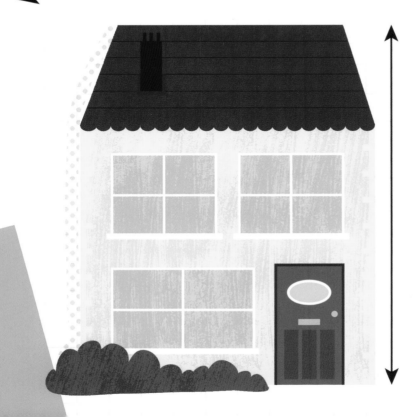

How do your estimates measure up?

Estimate : _____

# SHOPPING

Going shopping involves math! You need to add together your money to check you have enough to buy everything and to give the cashier the right amount.

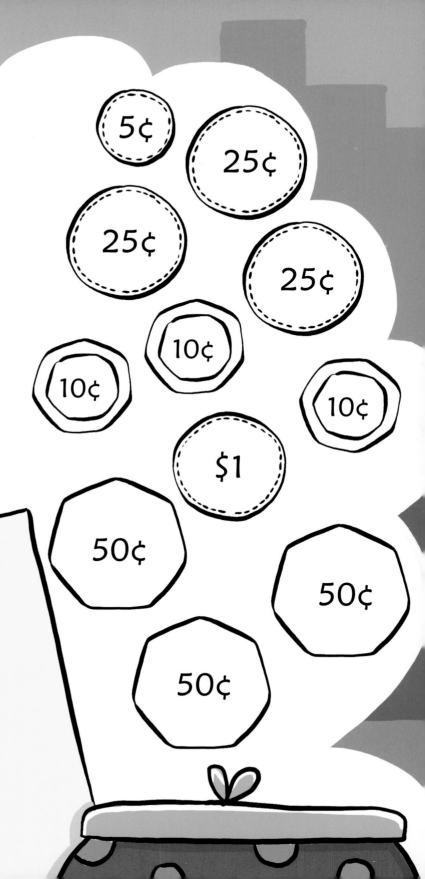

Check the prices of everything on your shopping list against the money you have in your pocket. On your shopping list, write down how much each will cost and which coins you'll need. Put a cross over each coin when you've used it.
Answers on page 126!

2 lemons

4 bananas

1 pint of milk

1 loaf of bread

3 apples

50¢
a pint

85¢

OPEN

25¢ each

25¢ each

25¢ each

103

# AT THE POST OFFICE

Bigger things aren't necessarily heavier than smaller things. A pillow filled with feathers is larger than a brick, but the brick is heavier. We can measure weight by using scales, and the metric scale measures in grams (g) and kilograms (kg). There are 1,000 grams in a kilogram.

Check the scales for each of these parcels and write their weights in the spaces provided. Answers on page 126! What do you think is in each box? Draw your answers!

Here are some sample weights to give you ideas. But you can also weigh items around you and choose things to put in the parcels that are not on this list.

Remember this little symbol?
≈

a packet of potato chips ≈ 35g
a tennis ball ≈ 50g
a DVD in its case ≈ 100g
a mobile phone ≈ 150g
a cricket ball ≈ 175g
an exercise book ≈ 200g
a football ≈ 440g
a small bag of sugar ≈ 500g

1.

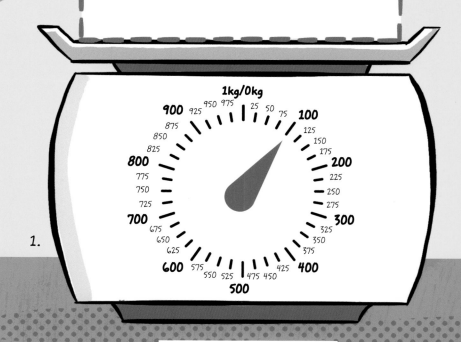

g

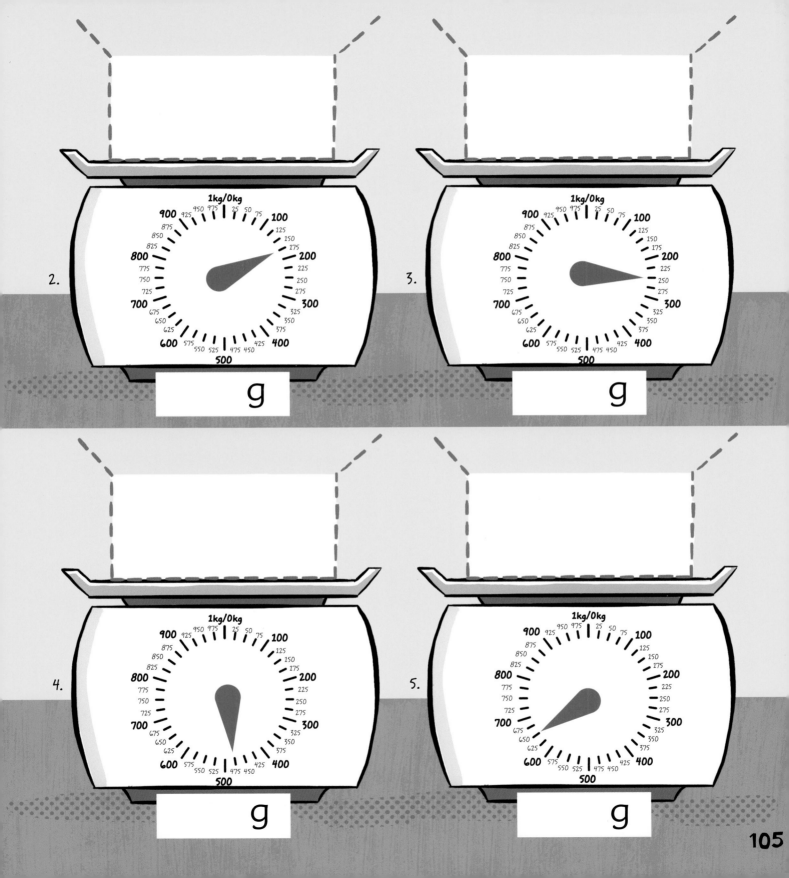

2. ____ g

3. ____ g

4. ____ g

5. ____ g

# TAKE AWAYS

Things are taken away – or subtracted – in all sorts of everyday situations. Some things are simple to count, if they are all the same size and shape, such as squares of a chocolate bar. Other things, like liquids, have to be measured in fractions (or equal parts) of a whole unit. The whole unit could be an official way of measuring, such as liters, or anything useful, like a bottle or cup.

For each of these objects, shade in the amount that has been taken away or used up, and write down the amount left.

Someone has eaten 7 squares.
Amount left: _____

A quarter of the bottle has been used.
Amount left: _____

6 pins have been knocked over
Amount left:

_____

106

Subtract all the spaces with a dot marked in them by coloring them in — and you'll find a picture revealed in the space left behind.

# VOLUME

Capacity – also called 'volume' – is a measure of how much space something takes up. You can measure the capacity of things that can be poured from one container to another. Capacity can be measured in milliliters (ml) and liters (l), and there are 1,000 milliliters in a liter. However, you might see capacity measured in all sorts of ways.

Here are some common ways capacity is measured:

 a pinch

 a drop

 a teaspoon

 a tablespoon

 a cup

In this recipe, some of the ingredients are measured in weight, and some are measured in volume. Circle the words that are telling you what volume to use.

Clue: Remember – volume isn't always measured in just milliliters and liters.

## Vanilla Cupcakes
4 oz./110g butter

4 oz./110g caster sugar

2 free-range eggs

1 teaspoon vanilla extract

4 oz./110g self-raising flour

1-2 tablespoons milk

## Buttercream icing
5 oz./140g butter

9 ¾ oz./280g icing sugar

1-2 tablespoons milk

a few drops food coloring

Decorate these cupcakes!

1. Preheat the oven to 180° C (350° F) and line a muffin tin with paper cases (ask an adult to help you).

2. Cream the butter and sugar together then slowly beat in the eggs and vanilla extract.

3. Carefully mix in the flour adding little drops of milk as you go.

4. Bake for 10-15 minutes until golden on top then leave to cool.

5. Beat the butter for the icing until soft then add half of the icing sugar and beat some more.

6. Add the rest of the icing sugar and the milk to the butter and mix until smooth.

7. Decorate your cupcakes! Use food coloring in the icing for a special finish.

# MULTIPLES

Multiplication is adding the same number to itself an amount of times. So, 3 x 3 means to add 3 to itself three times, or 3 + 3 + 3.

You can represent 3 x 3 in a grid, too, where there are 3 rows and 3 columns, like this:

or 2 x 4 like this:

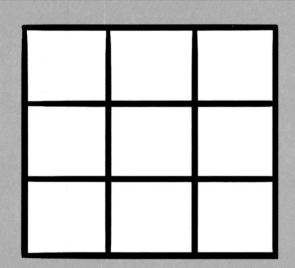

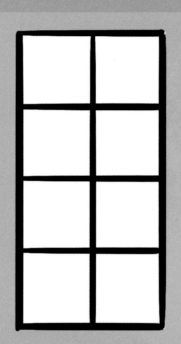

And counting the number of squares gives you the answer to the question.

Use the pictures opposite to help you solve these multiplication questions.
Look for the boxes that match the number of rows and columns in the question.

2 X 5 = ☐          5 X 6 = ☐

3 X 6 = ☐          8 X 9 = ☐

4 X 5 = ☐          9 X 10 = ☐

111

# RACING MATH

It's important to know how to measure time. Telling the time helps you arrive at school on time and helps your teacher make sure your lessons last the right amount of time. People running races also need to measure time to know exactly how long they have taken. Time can be measured in seconds, minutes and hours. There are 60 seconds in a minute and 60 minutes in an hour.

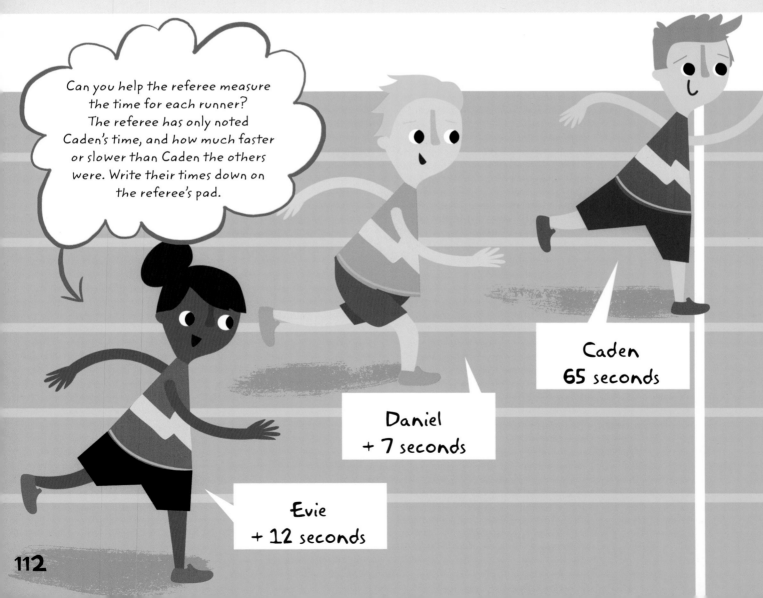

Can you help the referee measure the time for each runner? The referee has only noted Caden's time, and how much faster or slower than Caden the others were. Write their times down on the referee's pad.

Caden
65 seconds

Daniel
+ 7 seconds

Evie
+ 12 seconds

1st : Ahmed ———————————

2nd : Betty ———————————

3rd : Caden 1 minute 5 seconds

4th : Daniel ———————————

5th : Evie ———————————

# SHARING

Sharing things out is called 'division.' Things can be shared out evenly but sometimes there will be leftovers known as the remainder.

These cakes have all been cut into different numbers of slices. First, count the number of slices, then use different colored pencils to share out the slices equally amongst the number of guests listed for each cake. Each guest can have more than one slice of cake but they must all have the same number of slices each.
Here's one to start you off.

Number of slices: **8**
Share between **4** guests
Slices left over: **0**

Number of slices: _____

Share the slices between 6 guests

Slices left over: _____

Number of slices: _____

Share the slices between 4 guests

Slices left over: _____

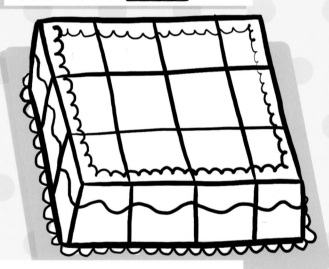

Number of slices: _____

Share the slices between 5 guests

Slices left over: _____

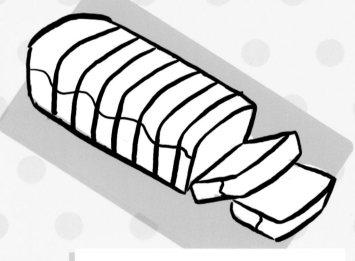

Number of slices: _____

Share the slices between 9 guests

Slices left over: _____

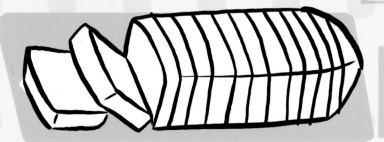

Number of slices: _____

Share the slices between 7 guests

Slices left over: _____

The clue's in the title! The code is simply the reverse of the alphabet. This code is easy to crack but that also means you'll never forget how to crack it, even if you lose your key.

| A | B | C | D | E | F | G | H | I | J | K | L | M | N | O | P | Q | R | S | T | U | V | W | X | Y | Z |
|---|---|---|---|---|---|---|---|---|---|---|---|---|---|---|---|---|---|---|---|---|---|---|---|---|---|
| Z | Y | X | W | V | U | T | S | R | Q | P | O | N | M | L | K | J | I | H | G | F | E | D | C | B | A |

| D | S | Z | G | | R | H | | U | L | I | | W | R | M | M | V | I | ? |
|---|---|---|---|---|---|---|---|---|---|---|---|---|---|---|---|---|---|---|
| | | | | | | | | | | | | | | | | | | |

## AUGUSTUS'S CODE

Another simple code, this time the alphabet is all shifted on one place, so that A=B, B=C, and so on until Z=A.
This message uses the bottom line of the code.

| A | B | C | D | E | F | G | H | I | J | K | L | M | N | O | P | Q | R | S | T | U | V | W | X | Y | Z |
|---|---|---|---|---|---|---|---|---|---|---|---|---|---|---|---|---|---|---|---|---|---|---|---|---|---|
| Z | A | B | C | D | E | F | G | H | I | J | K | L | M | N | O | P | Q | R | S | T | U | V | W | X | Y |

| Z | T | F | T | R | S | T | R | | V | Z | R | | Z | | Q | N | L | Z | M |
|---|---|---|---|---|---|---|---|---|---|---|---|---|---|---|---|---|---|---|---|
| | | | | | | | | | | | | | | | | | | | |

# PICTOGRAM CODE

You don't always need to use letters in your code!
Pictograms, or little pictures, can take the place of letters.

| B | C | D | E | F | G | H | I | J | K | L | M | N | O | P | Q | R | S | T | U | V | W | X | Y | Z |
|---|---|---|---|---|---|---|---|---|---|---|---|---|---|---|---|---|---|---|---|---|---|---|---|---|
| 👌 | 👍 | 👎 | 👉 | 👈 | ☝ | 🤙 | ✋ | ☺ | 😐 | ☹ | 💣 | ☠ | 🚩 | 🏴 | ✈ | ☀ | 💧 | ❄ | ✝ | ♰ | ☦ | ✠ | ✡ | ☾ |

| ✋ | 💧 |  | ❄ | 👍 | ✋ | 💧 |  | 👉 | ✌ | 💧 | ✡ |  | 🚩 | ☀ |  | 👎 | ✌ | ☀ | 👎 | ? |
|---|---|---|---|---|---|---|---|---|---|---|---|---|---|---|---|---|---|---|---|---|
|  |  |  |  |  |  |  |  |  |  |  |  |  |  |  |  |  |  |  |  |  |

Have a go at making your own code.
Fill in the empty boxes to give each letter a code, and then use your code to write a secret message! Don't forget to share the code with a partner so they can decipher your message.

| A | B | C | D | E | F | G |
|---|---|---|---|---|---|---|
|   |   |   |   |   |   |   |

| H | I | J | K | L | M | N |
|---|---|---|---|---|---|---|
|   |   |   |   |   |   |   |

| O | P | Q | R | S | T | U |
|---|---|---|---|---|---|---|
|   |   |   |   |   |   |   |

| V | W | X | Y | Z |
|---|---|---|---|---|
|   |   |   |   |   |

# TURN THE TABLES

Making notes of the things we see can helps us to see patterns. Writing stuff down helps us to take more notice.

Look at this scene and record information about it in the table by putting ticks in the right boxes. The first line has been filled in for you.

|  | mum | dad | brother | sister | baby |
|---|---|---|---|---|---|
| eating cereal |  |  | ✔ | ✔ | ✔ |
| eating toast |  |  |  |  |  |
| curly hair |  |  |  |  |  |
| straight hair |  |  |  |  |  |
| wearing red |  |  |  |  |  |
| smiling |  |  |  |  |  |
| drinking juice |  |  |  |  |  |
| drinking milk |  |  |  |  |  |

# BAR CHARTS

Tables gather numbers in a grid. Bar charts are a fun way to turn information into something visual. A 'bar' on the chart represents the number value in the table.

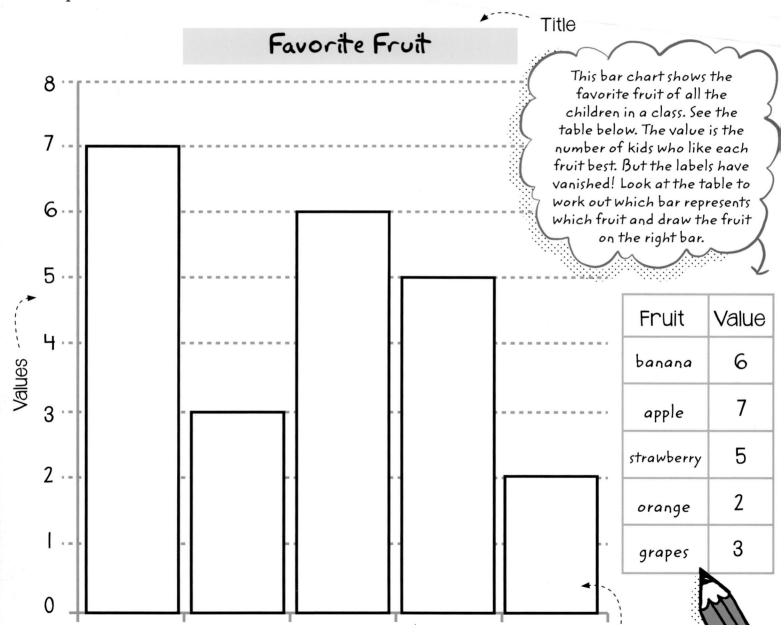

**Favorite Fruit**

Title

This bar chart shows the favorite fruit of all the children in a class. See the table below. The value is the number of kids who like each fruit best. But the labels have vanished! Look at the table to work out which bar represents which fruit and draw the fruit on the right bar.

| Fruit | Value |
|-------|-------|
| banana | 6 |
| apple | 7 |
| strawberry | 5 |
| orange | 2 |
| grapes | 3 |

Values

Labels

Bars

Victor gathered this information about his friends' favorite hobbies. Use a pencil and ruler to turn the information in this table into a bar chart.

| Hobby | Value |
|---------|-------|
| football | 8 |
| ballet | 4 |
| swimming | 5 |
| karate | 2 |
| scouts | 5 |

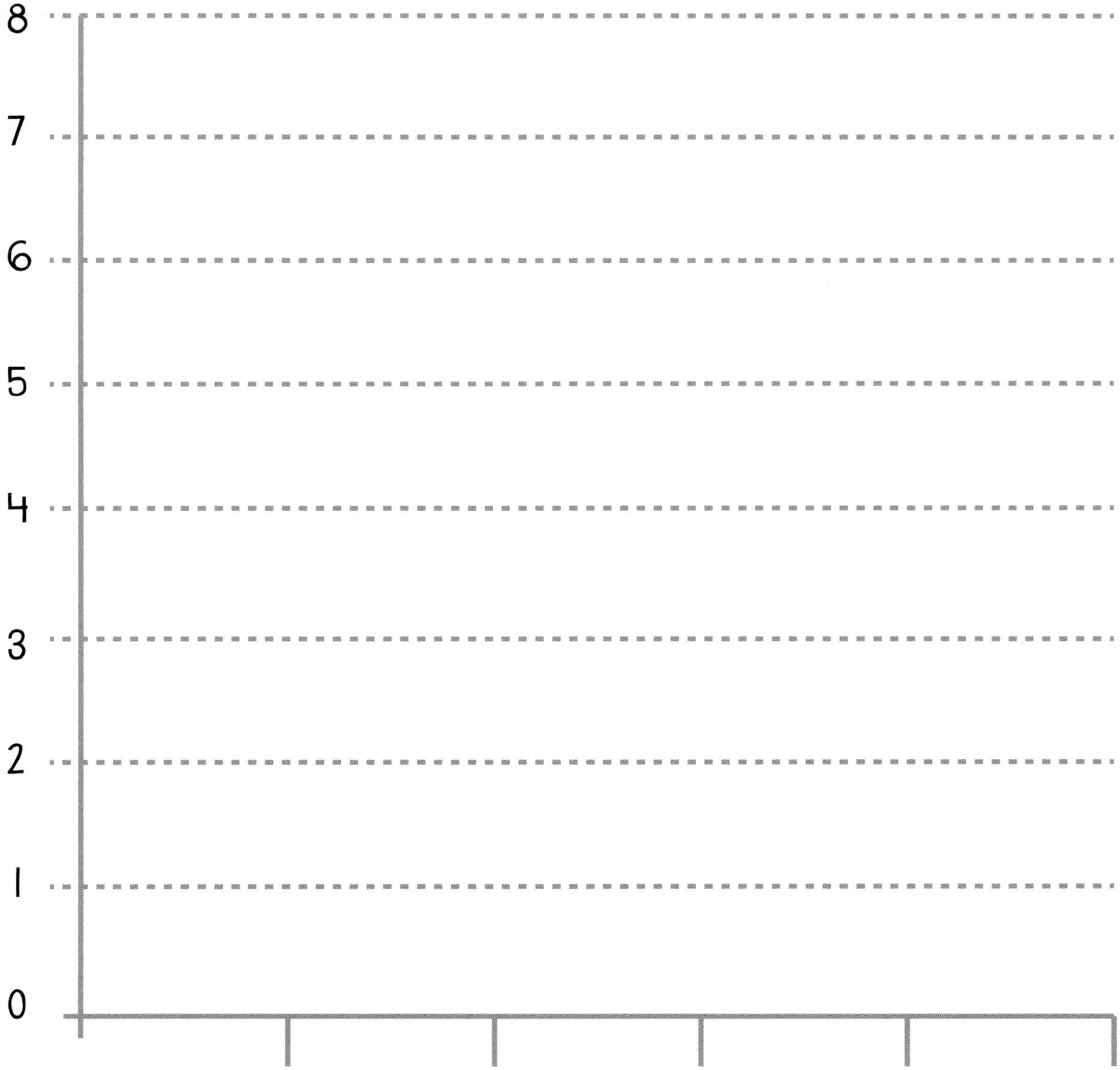

8

7

6

5

4

3

2

1

0

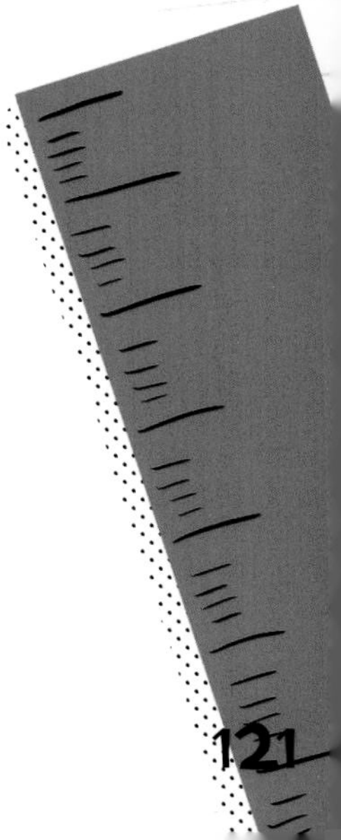

# RIGHT ANGLES

When two straight lines meet they make an angle. A 'right angle' is a special kind of angle, shaped like an 'L' – once you can recognize a right angle you'll see they are all around us.

See if you can find eight right angles in this picture. Circle all the ones you can find.

# ROUNDING UP

Sometimes it's easier to understand larger numbers if they are rounded up or down to something simpler.

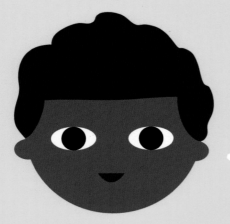

Numbers 1 to 4 are rounded down to the nearest 0. So 13 becomes 10.

Numbers 5 to 9 are rounded up to the nearest 0. So 27 becomes 30.

You can also round off numbers and use other words to describe numbers. Here are some words you can use to describe a number without saying the exact number.

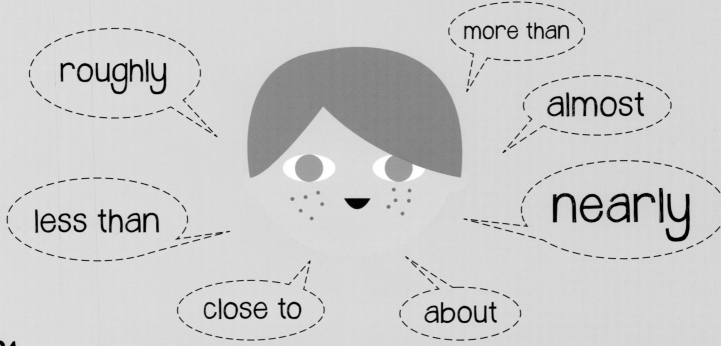

roughly

more than

almost

less than

nearly

close to

about

In these conversations, reply to the friend talking in exact numbers with another way of describing the number, rounded off. Use the words suggested on the opposite page to help you.

I have 97 action figures!

You have nearly 100 action figures!

I can skip 32 times without stopping!

I am 8 years and 11 months old.

I scored a basket 11 times in a row!

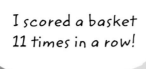

There are 26 pupils in my class.

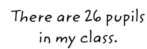

# ANSWERS

Pages 100-101

**Pencils**
Estimate : **6cm**
Measurement : **6.3 cm**

**Container of cherry tomatoes**
Estimate : **15cm**
Measurement : **15.3 cm**

**House**
Estimate : **6 m**

Pages 102-103

2 lemons = 50¢ (2 x 25¢)

4 bananas = $1 (1 x $1)

1 pint of milk = 50¢ (1 x 50¢)

1 loaf of bread = 85¢ (1 x 50¢, 1 x 25¢, 1 x 10¢)

3 apples = 75¢ (1 x 50¢, 2 x 10¢, 1 x 5¢)

Page 104-105

**Here are the weights showing on the scales and some ideas for what could be inside the parcels. You might have chosen other things to go in the parcels by weighing items around you.**

1. The scale shows 100g = a DVD in its case
2. The scale shows 175g = a cricket ball
3. The scale shows 250g = an exercise book + a tennis ball
4. The scale shows 475g = a football + a packet of crisps
5. The scale shows 650g = a small bag of sugar + a mobile phone

Page 106

| Chocolate bar | Bottle of laundry liquid | Bowling pins |
|---|---|---|
| Amount left: 23 | Amount left: ¾ | Amount left: 4 |

Page 107

Page 108-109

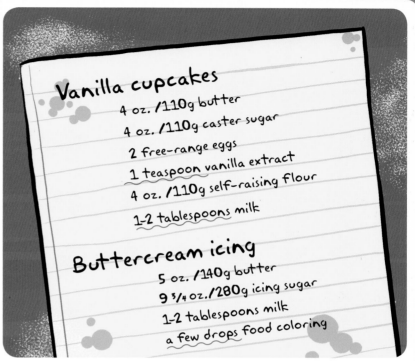

### Vanilla cupcakes

4 oz. /110g butter

4 oz. /110g caster sugar

2 free-range eggs

1 teaspoon vanilla extract

4 oz. /110g self-raising flour

1-2 tablespoons milk

### Buttercream icing

5 oz. /140g butter

9 ³/₄ oz. /280g icing sugar

1-2 tablespoons milk

a few drops food coloring

Page 110-111

$2 \times 5 = 10$

$3 \times 6 = 18$

$4 \times 5 = 20$

$5 \times 6 = 30$

$8 \times 9 = 72$

$9 \times 10 = 90$

Page 112-113

1st : Ahmed 55 seconds

2nd : Betty 1 minute

3rd : Caden 1 minute 5 seconds

4th : Daniel 1 minute 12 seconds

5th : Evie 1 minute 17 seconds

Page 114-115

Cake 1
Number of slices: 12
Slices left over: 0

Cake 2
Number of slices: 9
Slices left over: 1

Cake 3
Number of slices: 12
Slices left over: 2

Cake 4
Number of slices: 10
Slices left over: 1

Cake 5
Number of slices: 14
Slices left over: 0

Page 116-117

Reverse Alphabet: **What is for dinner?**

Augustus's Code: **Augustus was a Roman**

Pictogram Code: **Is this easy or hard?**

Page 118-119

|  | Mum | Dad | brother | sister | baby |
|---|---|---|---|---|---|
| eating cereal |  |  | ✔ | ✔ | ✔ |
| eating toast | ✔ | ✔ |  |  |  |
| curly hair | ✔ |  | ✔ |  |  |
| straight hair |  | ✔ |  | ✔ |  |
| wearing red | ✔ | ✔ |  |  | ✔ |
| smiling | ✔ |  | ✔ |  | ✔ |
| drinking juice |  |  | ✔ | ✔ | ✔ |
| drinking milk |  |  |  |  | ✔ |

Page 120-121

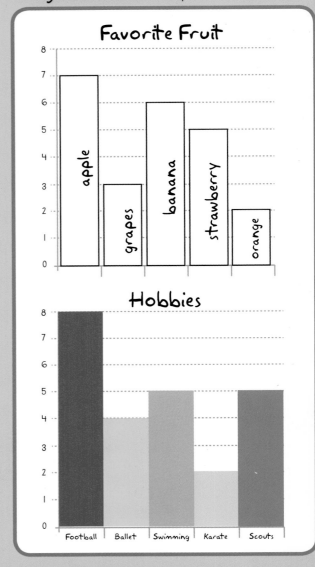

**Favorite Fruit**

**Hobbies**

Page 122-123

There are 8 right angles in the picture.

Page 124-125

**Possible answers:**

- You can skip more than 30 times!
- You are nearly 9 years old.
- You have scored more than 10 baskets in a row.
- You have close to 30 pupils in your class.